SUPER STAR
HIRING SYSTEM

*How to Easily
Attract, Screen & Hire
a Successful Superstar Team*

TRISH GRIMES

ꙮ STERLING PUBLISHING GROUP ꙮ

ເ8 SPG ຂ

Editor & Creative Director: Jodi Nicholson www.jodinicholson.com
Cover Design by the Artistic Team at Sterling Publishing Group
Photography by Mariusz Jeglinski

This book is a part of a collection from Trish Grimes Consulting, a
division of Ruby Studios, Inc., and may be ordered by contacting the
author at books@TrishGrimes.com or http://www.TrishGrimes.com

Published by
The Sterling Publishing Group, USA 813.720.7458
http://www.SterlingPublishingGroup.com

Printed in the United States of America
ISBN: 978-0-9884656-8-8

Business | Work Culture | Human Resources & Management

DEDICATION

This book is dedicated to the love of my life, my mom, Connie Grimes.

Everything that I am today is because of her belief in me, the sacrifices she made for me, and her unconditional love for me.

Today she is living with Alzheimer's and no longer recognizes me. But for the first 45 years of my life she gave me the strength and support to know that everything was possible!

I love you mom and I miss you every day.

- Trish Grimes

TABLE OF CONTENTS

SUPER STAR
HIRING SYSTEM

How to Easily
Attract, Screen & Hire
a Successful Superstar Team

TRISH GRIMES

1 | CULTURE

Let's kick it off and dig right in by starting with your company's culture. You might be wondering what does culture have to do with hiring?

The answer is EVERYTHING!

First, what is CULTURE?

In the business world, the reference name of "culture" is interchangeable yet has consistent qualities and may be called: Organizational Culture, Corporate Culture, Work Culture, Business Culture, or Company Culture.

The culture of your company encompasses the values, behaviors and attributes that make up the unique psychological and social aspects of the environment of the organization. Culture represents the values, principles and beliefs of the principles collectively within an organization, and includes the mission, values, vision, symbols, language, beliefs and habits of the team dynamics.

Now before you do ANYTHING, you must identify the culture of your company. Culture is primary and once defined it will help you to identify who fits in.

So let me ask you this ... If you're currently in business with a staff, have you ever hired a person only to find that they quit after a few months with no explanation at all?

And then what happened?

They seemed so excited to start, and it all seemed so good.

Hmm ... So what the heck?

Here's what happened. Here's what I know. They weren't a good fit for your corporate culture.

We see our workmates more than we see our family. Therefore, wouldn't it make sense that we should love that environment and thrive in it for those 10 hours a day?

For example, your business culture may be based on beliefs spelled out in your mission statement. Maybe it's a symbol, like the rainbow-colored apple that symbolizes Apple, Inc.

Regardless of the shape your logo or symbol takes, your company's culture plays a BIG role in determining how well your business will do.

Let's break it down.

Whether written as a mission statement, spoken or merely understood, corporate culture describes and governs the ways a company's owners and employees think, feel and act.

And with that being said, it's very important for you to understand that your corporate culture comes from you. From your passion, from your vision, for that desire to show the world what you can do. This is where the corporate culture begins. This is where your passion defines the perfect customer and perfect employee.

If you're not happy with your culture, or if you're confused about the culture, there are things you can do to start changing it NOW.

If you are starting your business, you're in the right place and can start fresh!

Here's a simple checklist to begin defining your culture.

First, I want you to:

- Look inside your company and look at each of your employees.

- Describe the characteristics of your team that makes them get along so well.

- What are the similarities that make them a team?

For example, consider the following:

Age
Background
Education
Ethnicity
Gender
Common interests
Personality

If you don't have a culture yet, or if you aren't inspired and happy with the one you do have, then go back to the first day that you decided that you wanted to have a business.

Create a list of the things that used to make you so passionate about the business when it was just an idea in your head. Think about what you wanted to create with this company. What were you trying to deliver? What service or product were you bringing to the marketplace and why?

At Ruby Makeup Academy (RMA), the executive team and I wanted to create a company for women where they felt pretty, and empowered, and sexy!

Our culture is based on that "feel good, I'm sexy, take over the world" mentality that empowers our team.

I want to share with you the characteristics of the **Ruby Corporate Culture** that I used to create a thriving, prosperous, INC 500/5000 company:

- We like to have a good time

- We like to make money, BIG MONEY!

- We work in a fast paced, high-pressure environment, and we HAVE FUN while doing it!

- The average age of our employee is 25

- The average manager's age is between 25-30

- Our employees are primarily female and Hispanic

- Everyone in the company is young, beautiful, enthusiastic, and they like each other!

- The team members are happy to see each other every day

- The team works hard toward a common goal

- We are a young, fun, energetic group of women that LOVE makeup!

I find that most of our employees were either cheerleaders, or played on a sports team when they were in school. Those two activities require high energy and solid teamwork. Also, people that participate in sports and cheer tend to have very high self-esteem. They possess core leadership qualities or, they are leaders.

Do you see where I'm going with this?

I can walk into any company in any city and tell you what the corporate culture is. First of all when you try to define corporate culture, take an honest hard look at yourself.

So now it's YOUR turn.

- What is YOUR corporate culture?
- Who are YOU?
- Tell me about YOUR company?
- What makes YOU tick?
- What's your passion?
- WHO works for you?

Go through your list of employees and profile them.

This will help to begin describing your company's culture.

Now, go back to the first day that you decided that you wanted to have a business.

I encourage you to create a list of the things that USED to make you so passionate about the business when it was just an idea in your head.

Think about what you wanted to create with this company... your dream business.

What service or product were you trying to deliver?

So here's your homework...

Go to the Internet and view the Corporate Culture of the following three companies: Google, Zappos, and Starbucks.

Starbuck's changed the way that we see coffee. They make us feel good about spending $5 for a cup of coffee while waiting in long lines just for the privilege of getting that delicious cup of Joe!

After researching their various cultures, you will have the ammunition that you need to sit down and thoroughly dissect your company to determine your own corporate culture.

Next I want you to outline your own corporate culture.

Ask yourself the following:

- What is MY environment?
- Describe it! Is it fun? Is it stuffy? Is it rigid?

Whatever the answers are, it's ok! There are NO wrong answers.

It's important to first define the environment that you are in. Once you find your environment, then you can define the type of person that will work in that environment.

For us, we have a young energetic company that revolves around makeup. It wasn't hard to figure out who wants to work with makeup... It's young females!

Next...

- What kind of business are YOU in?
- WHO wants to work there?

The first critical step in hiring is to take the time to do this process. If you DO, you will find that recruiting, hiring and team retention will become a natural and a painless part of your business.

Go do your homework and once you've completed it, come back and join me in the next chapter where we will create the avatar of your next, ideal SUPERSTAR hire!

2 | CREATING A SUPERSTAR AVATAR

In the first chapter I asked you to research some of America's top leaders that have changed how we view corporate culture: Google, Zappos and Starbucks.

I also asked you to define YOUR corporate culture and what type of person is best suited to work in your company. Did you?

If you know the answers, sit tight! If you STILL don't know the answers then it's time for a field trip.

Here we go!

Figure out what business you are in, or what business you want to be in. Maybe you are wanting to start a new business but haven't quite figured out how to do it.

As part of that process you have to establish early on who will work in your company. Determine what business you are in and create a list of other similar businesses in the marketplace. Most of the time there will be other companies doing something similar to what you are doing or similar to what you aspire to do as a company.

When Ruby Polanco and I first created Ruby Cosmetics, we knew that we were creating a business that was geared towards females. Beyond that, Ruby, a Latina herself, was actually creating a line of makeup that was specifically geared toward Hispanic women, because at that time, no one was gearing their product line towards a clientele that has yellow skin undertones; and so we went after *that* market.

Knowing what our product launch would be and who our target market was, we had to decide the best medium to launch the sales and distribute the product. We decided to launch through a kiosk in a mall. After that we spent many months walking malls in Southern California to determine where our first kiosk should be, we ultimately picked the Westfield shopping center in West Covina, CA due to its extremely heavy Hispanic demographics.

So there we were in West Covina getting ready to launch a brand new makeup line. We literally sat in the mall and watched the traffic. We walked the mall and looked at the clientele and the sales people at the other makeup counters.

Through our observations, we immediately were able to determine that the right employee for our company would be female, under 25 years old, and very likely Hispanic... And ten years later, that profile remains consistent of the Ruby Girl!

Before you can create your avatar, you MUST clearly identify your potential customers and employees.

Remember like attracts like.

People like to buy from people that they like. We are all attracted to mirror images of ourselves!

I'm going to talk a lot in this section about your customers: past, present and future, because your customers and your employees are actually the same person.

Here's some valuable information for our market. 95% of our Ruby Girls started out in the classroom as students of RMA. Who else is more passionate about your business than a raving fan? No one! Knowing this, and hiring our raving fans, we have created a multimillion dollar, INC 500 Company.

You have to analyze your customers' ages, locations, lifestyles, ethnicity, hobbies, financial situations, etc.

This is why you need an AVATAR!

What is an AVATAR you ask?

An avatar is a fictitious person created by you, who embodies your ideal customer and employee.

Here's why an avatar will benefit your business:

You can fine-tune your marketing message, and by marketing I mean connecting with your target via email, Facebook ads, Websites, Blogs, Podcasts, YouTube, Snapchat, Livestreams, Twitter, Instagram and all other media platforms ... EVERYTHING! Your future employee already follows you on Facebook, Instagram, Twitter, Pinterest, etc.

When the words and images on your page are directed TOWARDS your avatar, your target customers and employees will get the impression that you're talking DIRECTLY to them and addressing their specific needs, which means they're far more likely to show interest to buy from and work for you.

Creating an avatar is about going deep into their lives, their interests, their fears, their desires, the words they use and the phrases they simply don't understand. When you're starting up your business, you need to think about both the niche market you are in and your avatar.

How to create an avatar

Imagine you're introducing your avatar to a good friend, in a lot of great detail!

Create a "Day in the Life" of the avatar!

It may seem silly, but it will make this process SO much easier.

Here are 3 steps to think about:

Step 1: Your avatar's demographic

- Where do they live?
- What do they look like? (Height, weight, hair, ethnicity, clothing, shoes, etc.)
- How old are they?
- What do they do for a living?
- What do they do for fun?
- What kind of personality do they have? (Fierce, friendly, uptight, funny, quiet, shy, etc.)

Step 2: Define your avatar's needs:

- What's their biggest desire?
- What's their biggest problem?
- How can you help them RIGHT NOW?

Step 3: Where to find your avatar:

- What websites or blogs do they read?
- Who do they follow on Instagram?
- What pages do they "like" on Facebook?

- What kind of information do they search for?
- Do they watch YouTube videos? (If so, what do they watch?)

So what do you think?

I think you will need to repeat and process this chapter several times, brainstorm and take lots of notes!

This process is important and it's REALLY intense, however, stick with it, fine-tune it and be a superstar! Remember to be thorough, yet please be patient with yourself as well because your avatar WILL determine the course of your business and your hiring patterns forever. This took us YEARS to brand ourselves and create the Ruby Girl avatar. It doesn't happen overnight. But now that we have her ... *The Ruby Girl!* We never and I mean NEVER deviate from her. This is one of the most important things you will ever do for your business... creating your *Superstar Avatar.*

Ok, it's homework time! It's time for YOU to create your own avatar!

Good luck, work hard, and get crystal clear now!

3 | YOUR CULTURE & ENVIRONMENT

How did your AVATAR turn out? Can you clearly describe your ideal person to ME? To your market? To your candidates, potential employees, teammates and/or clients?

Yes!

Then do it ... Describe your avatar!

- Age?
- Ethnicity?
- Gender?
- Where do they live?
- What's their income?
- What do they watch on YouTube?
- Are they on Facebook or Instagram?
- What else, specifically, did you add?

Great! You get the idea.

I want to touch on ethnicity for just a minute as I do reference it throughout this book. We are not trying to racially profile, nor do we suggest it. However, with that said, in **marketing** we can't deny the cultural differences and how they play out in corporate America as we assess buying patterns. For Ruby Cosmetics and Ruby Makeup Academy (RMA), we've always known that the target market – the primary client, student and/or employee – is age 18-30, female and very likely Hispanic.

Does that mean that we only have 25 year old Latina's in the classroom and on payroll? No, of course not.

Statistically, 90% of our students and employees do fit the profile of our avatar.

If you are in a business that can capture the attention of the entire world, like Starbuck's or McDonald's, then great for you!

However, for most of us, we have to focus our marketing efforts on a specific target audience, aka the AVATAR.

What does environment have to do with corporate culture? Well, you guessed it... EVERYTHING!

At RMA when we are hiring we have to be extra careful that the person is the right CULTURAL fit because they may end up in a 3-pack of cubicles TOGETHER!

Let me expand on this TG concept of *Cultural Togetherness* ... What is culture if not the environment that we surround ourselves with? As we look from country to country we see different cultures. Look at Asia, Africa, Europe, and North America, where we live. We are all so different and we all come from and are immersed into our own set of cultures and values.

I myself am a second generation Mexican-American. My mother is first generation Mexican-American and my father's ancestors were from Germany and Ireland. So I'm

13

a mixed batch of various nationalities that have come to America and blended into the melting pot of what is now American society. That's pretty common today. America is so diverse. Our ancestors have come from all over the world to create a better life for generations to come.

It's exactly the same for a corporate culture. You as the owner have so many choices when you start out. Do you run your business like Google, with no walls, employees hanging around an open area with laptops sitting on bouncy balls instead of chairs? Or, do you run it like a law firm with many walls and lots of closed doors. Or, is it something in between or something different all together?

At RMA it's kind of a cross between a law firm and Google. The Branch Managers have private offices but their doors are always open unless they are in a meeting. Some of the branches have private offices for the top producers. The Admissions Counselors usually sit together in bullpen-style cubicles. We built it this way for a few reasons:

1. Budget - Obviously because it was cheaper to put 3 people per office versus private offices for everyone.

2. Accountability - Our Admissions Counselors are sales people and they need to be dialing out, receiving calls or meeting with prospects and touring the campus.

   • If they aren't doing one of those things, they aren't working.

   • When someone sits alone in an office, it's easy to zone out and start surfing the

Internet, texting, NOT being productive, etc.

- When they sit together its harder to sit there and do nothing while the other two people are dialing out, taking calls, and talking to prospects.

3. Comradery - We as humans are basically social people. We need other humans around us in society to talk to, laugh with, go to lunch, etc.

   - A cubicle setting forces people out of their comfort zone and makes them interact with the other staff members in a very close and confined way. If you don't like your cubicle mate, it's going to be a long 40 hour week and so you figure out ways to make your life in the cubicles happy.

4. Goals and Rewards - When an Admissions Counselor starts out in a cubicle with two other cube mates, she wants to work hard to be the best and hopefully get a private office. Once she has that office, she wants to work hard to show management that she is qualified and capable. Now she is setting her sights on getting a big corner office as a Manager.

Culture is difficult to define, but you generally know when you have found an employee who appears to fit your culture. They just feel right. They fit into the dynamics of the organization YOU have created!

Culture IS the environment that surrounds you while at work all of the time. It's a POWERFUL element that:

- Determines your work enjoyment,
- Forms your work relationships, AND
- Ultimately determines if you will be successful in this job or not

How many times have you heard someone playfully make the comment, *"Oh this is my work husband or work wife?"*

Work is where we spend most of our time in life. The work environment absolutely has to be a fit for our personality or else we won't stay. In our company the Ruby Girls become such a great family. I see them all the time on Instagram and Facebook, out together on the weekend, at parties, at clubs, out to lunch, and generally just having a great time. We have created such a cohesive, fun, family environment that it extends beyond the walls of the corporate office and out into their personal lives.

In many ways, culture is like personality.

In a person, their personality is made up of values, beliefs, interests, experiences, upbringing, and habits.

It's the same for a business. The culture is made up of all of the life experiences each employee brings to work.

Culture is especially influenced by the owner(s), and the management team. Of course WE, as owners create the cultural environment that makes us happy.

I owned a mortgage company for 20 years before switching gears and creating Ruby Cosmetics. I'm used to working in an office with lots of noise and stress all around me, with deadlines looming over head and with something REALLY bad always about to happen!: Did interest rates go up? Was the loan locked? Did the deal fall out of escrow? This was MY environment for 20 years!

So when Ruby and I created the new company we wanted something more fun and vibrant! We thought: "Let's create a space where people actually WANT to come to work," instead of the usual... "Oh my GAWD, it's Monday morning!"

For the Ruby Girls, they get up every morning, put on a cute outfit, do their hair and makeup and feel pretty!

One of the things I hear over and over from our staff is how they love that they get to feel pretty at work. So frequently and in most businesses, the work environment **doesn't** lean towards beauty in the workplace. While at RMA, it's mandatory. The environment requires that they must walk through that door in a FULL state of glam before they can even clock in! It's the AVATAR and the CULTURE and the tone of the ENVIRONMENT!

What's YOUR environment?

What's mandatory?

Culture in the work environment can be seen by looking at the employees:

- language
- decision making
- education
- stories
- daily work practices

Something as simple as the things that people put on their desk or stick to their cubicle wall will tell you a lot about how employees view and participate in office culture. It all creates the environmental flow. The way that employees interact with each other at meetings and speak with each other all creates the environment that becomes part of your company culture.

Currently, we have four locations and at RMA we have a company wide staff meeting every Friday morning. We meet at the same campus because it's centrally located in the center of all of our locations.

All meetings start at 10:00 am sharp, no exception. So at 10:00 am without fail every Friday, we crank up the music and have everyone get on their feet and dance! We all dance one song together.

I hear people say, *"I don't know how to dance, and I don't like to dance, blah blah blah!"*

And I say, *"I don't care ... Get on your feet and move! Jump! Get your body moving and shake it out!"*

By the end of the song, everybody has done about three minutes of cardio and is smiling and laughing and ready to start an upbeat meeting. It creates a fun, productive, energized environment.

By the way, when I walk in the door I've *already* worked out with my trainer and I'm in a pumped state so I get my girls on their feet and we do our 3 minutes of dance moves cardio mix!

I encourage you to bring some upbeat energy into your meetings, and use my format at your next staff meeting. Bring a great boom box so you can really crank up the volume for maximum effect. You will see that your staff is ready to listen and participate in this environment much more so than when you just walk into the room cold and start talking at them. Also, be sure to design an environment to create an effective flow that best works for your business.

At RMA our girls have to look fierce: hair, makeup, nails and wardrobe. When you walk through the front door of any campus the music is blaring. That's the environment that we created to attract the 18-25 year olds. Our avatar wants to see BEAUTIFUL women working, and they love to hear music blasting through the hallways. It makes them feel comfortable and right at home. They relax into that environment while they wait for their Admissions Counselor.

So I ask again, what is your environment?

What does your avatar want to see when they walk in your front door?

When you answer this, you will have answered these questions:

- What IS or should be my environment?
- What does my avatar want?

For all businesses there must be accountability in order to have success. When we have employees we must create the environment of accountability with a reward and demerit system. In ALL forms of society there has to be laws. It's the same inside of each business. There MUST be laws that we all follow in order to be successful.

We live in a world that is now dominated by social media. As a small business person, you have to create an environment that is pleasing to your avatar. Social media can make or break any small business with just a stroke of the keyboard. Given the impact of social media we simply CANNOT tolerate poor performance from our employees. You MUST create the environment that makes your avatar happy. Of course we can't please ALL of the people ALL of the time but as a business owner, you should be pleased with your team, your culture and your environment.

Culture is learned.

People LEARN to perform certain behaviors through either rewards or consequences.

At RMA we believe strongly in the recognition and reward system.

Culture is learned through interaction. Employees learn culture by interacting with other employees in the work environment.

It's like when we were kids and would say: "monkey see...monkey do!" It's the same in the work environment; employees watch each other. They see that hard work equals rewards. They also see that bad behavior equals termination! Employees learn culture by interacting with other employees.

When someone comes into your place of business to apply for a job, they already have a sense of your culture. The first opinion of your culture is formed the very first time that they see you on the Internet, call you or walk in your door. I encourage you to be wise about how your company is represented. For us, the receptionist is one of the most critical hires in the company.

Remember this... You NEVER have a second chance to make a good first impression!

Ok, now its time for some homework.

I simply want you to think about your environment so here are a few ideas to trigger your brain.

Think about...

- Who works there?
- Are they young or old
- Is it multi cultural

- Are there multiple languages spoken?
- Where is it?
- Big City?
- Small town?
- What kind of space is it?
- Private Office?
- Cubicles?
- Retail?
- Food Service?

So pencil out some ideas, brainstorm and get clear on your environment! Then, get ready for the next chapter where we'll be talking about recruiting and the resources to find your avatar.

4 | RESOURCES TO FIND YOUR AVATAR

I just want to ask: Did you take the time to pencil out some ideas about your environment?

Did you get clear?

Yes?

I thought so! Now that you've identified your avatar and your environment, it's time to get into the meat of this course ... RECRUITING!

I LOVE recruiting! Especially at RMA where I get super excited to meet all the new Ruby girls and guys!

Recruiting can be one of 2 things:

- If you do it RIGHT, you can have fun in the process and hire some pretty great people.
- If you do it wrong, it WILL BE your greatest challenge and worst nightmare!

Trust me; I know. I've experienced BOTH of those things in my business!

Hiring is an inevitable part of owning a business. You have to hire in order to grow. Your employees — being humans themselves — always have one eye open to see if the grass might be greener somewhere else. It's the natural evolution of business that employees will come and go, no matter how much you love them.

So now that we know **WHO** your avatar is, let's go out and find them.

The resources are right at your fingertips!

My first choice for a job post is always on social media if you use it for your business. When I post a job on social media, I ask them to respond to me via social media. If an ad is posted on Instagram or Facebook, I'll ask them to send me a private message inside Facebook. This gives me a chance to actually SEE the person so that I can get a feel for who they REALLY are. I ask for people to write to me and tell me WHY they would be great for this job.

Social media provides a CRITICAL examination tool. You'll find out more in 60 seconds on Facebook than you can learn in a 60-minute interview. When people are on Facebook they don't realize that a prospective employer might be looking. They are just living their life out loud and having a great time. And that's what I want to see ... How they live when no-one is looking!

Often times the way that people behave on a job interview is uptight, scared, nervous, and trying to make a good first impression. That's not who they REALLY are!

Social media depicts who they REALLY are, for better or for worse!

My "Ah-ha" moment in recruiting came when I asked my 23 year-old son, "If YOU were looking for a job *(and you are supposed to be looking for a job),* where would you go? What would you do?

He said, "I'd go to the Internet and type in: Job search Los Angeles."

This bit of information CHANGED the course of our hiring practices FOREVER!

So I went to the Internet and typed: Job search Los Angeles. The first thing that came up was Indeed.com — It's a National job database. I took a look around at the site and really I liked it. So when I want to post a classified ad, that's where I go! It's a very handy resource that I recommend, and one that you can clearly describe the position and the person you're looking for!

Now I want to touch base on your ABSOLUTE greatest recruiting tool of all time ... **Your current employees!**

Nobody, and I mean NOBODY, knows the profile of your avatar better than an existing avatar.

I offer all of my employees a referral fee for sending me a new hire. I pay out the referral fee AFTER the new hire passes their 90-day probation.

So let's recap my top three resources to find your avatar:
- Social media
- Indeed.com
- Employee referrals

The bottom line to all of this falls back on KNOWING your avatar. Once you know your avatar and I mean *really know your avatar*, you will know where to find them.

Your homework today is to go out and find a real live human avatar that fits your mold and ask them this question, "If you were looking for a job right now, what would YOU do?"

So go out and do your homework, and have fun with it! Then, we'll continue in the next chapter and learn another key ingredient ... *The Process of Elimination*.

5 | PROCESS OF ELIMINATION

In this chapter we are going to take a look at the *Process of Elimination*. I'm going to teach you a step-by-step system that will guide you through the process so easily that you might actually start to LIKE being a job recruiter. And in reality — as a business owner — aren't we ALL job recruiters?

I used to HATE hiring until I came up with this magic formula. Now, it's one of my favorite points in the recruiting process: The elimination process!

For us at RMA, the very best job candidates will come either from employee referrals or from social media. Remember, social media only works for recruiting if you already use it for your business. If you have big numbers and a lot of followers, social media is your best resource!

When I post an ad using social media, I require for them to send me a message via Facebook (FB). This way I can get inside of their personal page and look around.

Are they happy people?

Is it an image that would represent MY Company?

Are they the poster child of my avatar?

At this point you might be saying: What if I don't use social media?

Well, in that case, simply use another of my top resources that I shared in the last chapter. I would suggest posting on one of my favorite recruiting sites: INDEED.COM

It is our first and ONLY option for classified advertising.

- It has a good strong talent pool
- It's affordable
- You will spend $300 and get about 200 resumes.

Before you begin the screening process you need to create four (4) folders for your desk:

- YES
- TO CALL
- LEFT MESSAGE
- NO!

Now that your folders are ready to go here is my **Secret Formula for Screening Success** *along with my signature* **TG Hot Tips!**

This system is utilized foremost when you have place a classified ad. With an online ad, the resume lands in my inbox and I preview the resume on the computer.

1) The **FIRST STEP** is to **LOOK FOR RELEVANCE** ...

- Does their job history match OUR requirements
- Do they job hop?
- Does it feel like they could be my avatar?
- Where do they live?
- Is their resume well presented

TG's Hot Tip ... *Note, I spend less than 1 minute per resume on the initial scan.*

Continuing on with my secret formula ...

2) Next, my goal is to look at each resume as it comes across my desk. I give it a **QUICK SCAN** and decide **YES** or **NO!**

TG's Hot Tip ... *I get to the resumes as quickly as I can because they are HOT prospects.*

- For the ones that I reject – the **NO's** - I create an inbox called *RESUMES* and I drag the prospects into the folder to save and keep on file for 90 days.
- If the answer is **YES** move on to the next step.

3) YES ... PRINT IT and put it in the **TO CALL** folder.

4) Make your **CALLS**

Let's talk about the **CALLS**. I'd say that about 50% of the resumes that come to me feel like they MIGHT be qualified. So that's still a mission to make all those calls and have conversations with prospects, right? No, it's not and here's why.

A live person will answer only 50% of the calls you make. The other 50% will go to voicemail and file in the **LEFT MESSAGE** folder. Out of the messages you leave, less than 50% will call back!

Crazy! *Right?*

It's true! When I do get an actual live prospect, I introduce my company and myself. I tell them that I just received their resume. They are usually REALLY excited to hear from me and so glad that I called. Then, I hit them up with my secret weapon!

5) My Secret Weapon - Our CONVERSATION ...

I simply say: *"Tell me a little bit about YOURSELF."*

At this point, I have a headset on, I'm listening with INTENTION and I'm writing fast and furious, making relevant notes on their resume during the screening call.

TG's Hot Tip ... DO NOT make any notes that you wouldn't want to share in front of a labor board review! You will be sued for discrimination in hiring practices if there are notes on your resume that indicate anything about race, religion, etc. Remember you CANNOT ask if they are married, have children or how old they are! They might tell you, but YOU can't ask!

6) And lastly, you'll **FORM a PRELIMINARY DECISION** about the candidate based upon your screening call. At this time you'll either want to *eliminate* them or *invite them to proceed*. This final step for the screening process is covered in the next chapter, the interview process, along with conversation tips I use during the call.

Before we move forward into the final phase of the screening process and into the interview process, it's time for a little homework!

Your homework ...

First, decide if you have a large enough social media following AND if you can use it as an employment job board. Jot down some ideas *relevant* to your avatar or the position. Think about ways to connect with them on social media.

Second, think about creating a referral program for your current employees. How much is a high quality referral worth to YOU?

Third, take a look at www.Indeed.com and decide if it's right for you. If not, I encourage you to check out other online resources to determine the best fit for YOUR corporate culture.

Okay, you better get to it!

6 | THE INTERVIEW PROCESS

Everything we have done thus far from defining our culture, creating our avatar, recruiting and selecting potential candidates through the screening process has led us to the final phase of my *Secret Formula for Screening Success and the Interview Process!*

I told you that I usually have a live conversation with about 50% of all applicants that I screen. When I get them on the phone I simply say, *"Tell me about yourself."*

This totally catches them off guard. It's my secret weapon to job interviewing and now it can be your secret weapon too!

Remember, you need to be wearing a headset and have their resume in front of you. Take notes fast and furious. Note taking is a MUST! Otherwise at the end of the day, these 100+ resumes on your desk will ALL look the same!

As they are talking I'm listening to the words they say, the stories they tell and the *WAY* they say it.

I'm listening on *intention!*

Are they happy? Are they depressed? Did you wake them up at one o'clock in the afternoon? Do they sound high? Ha ha ha! You might laugh, but you are calling them in the middle of the day without notice, so don't be surprised by ANYTHING!

I'm looking for someone with confidence and clarity in their voice.

I much prefer to hire someone that already has a job versus someone that's currently unemployed. When you look at the resume, see if they are currently working or unemployed. How long have they been unemployed? I know it's a tough economy - It ALWAYS is! But there's usually a reason that someone is unemployed and the longer they are unemployed the more depressed they are, and the harder it is to get back into the swing of things when they re-enter the job force.

I'd much rather hire someone that already has a job and let them give their 2-week notice.

When you do hire someone that has a job, watch how they exit that job. Did they give proper notice OR did they quit today so they could start with you tomorrow? Whatever they did with their past employer is exactly how they will behave when it's time to exit your company!

TG's Hot Tip ... I actually won't hire someone if they currently have a job and tell me, *"It doesn't matter; they don't need me to give notice."* I can already see how their future will play out with US!

So right now, I'm in the screening process with hundreds of resumes, making my preliminary decision and doing phone interviews with my **YES** and **TO CALL** folders. I also have my original **NO** folder on my desk and a **NEW folder** I just added named **SKYPE**.

SKYPE? You must be thinking "WHAT the WHAT?"

Yes, Skype! This is another technique that I've implemented with great success — one that just isn't used for hiring. Until now! You and I are creating a SUPERSTAR HIRING REVOLUTION!

Sometimes I look at a resume and I'm concerned about job qualifications, duties, etc. But a lot of times, I'm not concerned about any of that.

I hire for a lot of entry-level sales and administrative positions. Sometimes I like to train people from scratch so that they don't come with any previous conceptions of *"at my other job, this is how we did it"* — NO!

So I'm listening to the flow and the stories and making notes. At the end of the conversation, I'll say one of two things:

- "Thank you for your time. I'm talking to a couple hundred people this week, taking notes and I'll pass all of the files on to the hiring manager."
- "I'd like to invite you to do a Skype interview with me."

The first sentence is my internal code for **NO!** In other words, ELIMINATED during the screening process and they are filed in the NO folder.

TG's Hot Tip ... I mentioned this in the previous chapter and want to reiterate that you must keep **all** resumes received for a period of 90 days *and* be able to produce your original copy along with notes, if requested by your governing labor board. Always follow the law provided by your governing labor board first!

Okay, back to the conversation ... if I say the second sentence, I'm inviting them to PROCEED in the interview process with a VIDEO CHAT via Skype. I'll be covering the specific details in the next chapter!

For now, we've gotten to the end of the telephone screening interview process and my *Secret Formula for Screening Success*. Applicants are either falling into the **NO**'s and the remaining candidates being invited to **SKYPE** with me.

How cool is that? COOL!

I realize it may sound like a lot a work upfront, however, here's where we have a critical choice to consider when valuing our company culture, time, current employees and our customers.

Each candidate if hired will have an impact on our business. I want Superstars, do you?

The big question is this: Do we put in the extra time and effort NOW — in the hiring process — or do we put in the time by hiring, training, firing, and then doing it all over again?

Let's do it NOW! Remember, this is *TG's Superstar Hiring System*!

Your homework in preparation for the next chapter is to set yourself up with the ability to video chat. I recommend Skype and you can download the app for free at https://www.skype.com/en/. It is the most widely used means of video chat on the market today.

7 | VIDEO CHAT INTERVIEW

By now, you should have your Skype account set up and ready to go for video chat! Please don't skip this critical step in the process and the *Superstar Hiring System*. It is what separates US from the pack. And now it will separate YOU from the pack too!

When I invite them to do a Skype interview with me, I schedule the video chats 15 minutes apart.

This face-to-face video chat is so critical. It truly separates the weak from the strong. It will tell me so much about the candidate. Now if your candidates don't have the ability to video chat, I recommend that you just scratch them off the list. In a recent round of interviews, I had one candidate go out and buy a video camera and install it to her desktop AND set up a Skype account just for the interview!

It always comes back to this ... how BADLY do they want the job? I only want the most highly motivated people to move on to the final round.

Here are some things to consider about your candidates when video chat is used for interviews.

- Some of them will be at home, in a quiet place, ready to go and wearing a suit. THESE are the smart ones! They KNOW it's a job interview!
- Some of them don't quite figure it out. These are the ones that show up without makeup and wearing a   T-Shirt or pajamas!
- Some of them are on the go but know they have an interview lined up so they will be ready wherever they are. They will take the interview from their car or any quiet place they can find.
- How badly do they want THIS job? That's what you have to ask yourself.
- What are they willing to DO? Are they willing to put on a suit and makeup to Skype from home on their day off?

What I'm looking for is:

- How do they look? Hair, makeup, wardrobe, etc.
- How do they speak?
- WHAT do they have to say?
- How is their posture?
- How is their energy?

During this process, I control the interview with a series of questions related to the specific position and their qualifications. In our phone interview I already had them tell me about themselves. Now that we are on video, I have my computer or iPad in front of me so my hands are free to write.

Remember, this is a face-to-face interview so I encourage you to spend more time looking at the candidate than writing with your head down. I'm referencing their resume and my notes to ask them questions during the interview, not reading it as I like to make eye contact with the candidate and have engaging conversation.

I'm looking for their answers but mostly I just want to see them speak and flow. I'm looking at their face and body language the entire time.

The process is usually less than 10 minutes and then I make my final notes and get ready for the next candidate.

When I'm done with the interview I will say one of two things:

- "Thank you for your time. I will pass my notes onto the hiring manager."
- "I'd like to invite you to come in for a live interview."

At this point, I have two folders in front of me:

- NO!
- LIVE INTERVIEW

Yes! I added another folder and it's one step closer to HIRING A SUPERSTAR!

8 | THE LIVE INTERVIEW

You can see that the candidates have gone through a lot just to get this point, and once a candidate has passed the Skype session, they are invited to meet with us live and in person.

We schedule 15 minute blocks of time and will meet with every job candidate, back-to-back, all in one day. In my organization the live interview panel consists of myself, Ruby and the manager that will directly supervise the new hire. This is our " HR Team" and I encourage you to have multiple team members present for the live interview to add depth, perspective and perception.

By the time the candidate is meeting live in front of us, I really don't have any more questions. I have asked everything by this time! I simply want to meet them in person and get a feel for who they really are, how they feel, assess their energy level and make a decision as to whether or not they truly fit the company culture. Every team has its unique quirks. I can have the most qualified candidate in front of me but if they don't fit the corporate culture, it's not a good hire and it simply won't work out.

I have the candidate tell us a little bit about themselves to get the ball rolling. Each member of the panel has specific questions for the candidate. And we just flow with the conversation and ask questions as they come to mind.

Some of the key questions that we like to ask:

- Tell me what you know about OUR company.
- Tell me WHY you want to work HERE.

You will be blown out by how many people make it this far in the process and don't know a DAMN thing about our company!

To us and RMA, that's an epic fail.

For what we put them through to make it in front of this panel, they had better have researched the hell out of this company and know everything there is to know!

I'm serious!

HOW BADLY DO THEY WANT THIS JOB?

We only allocate 15 minutes for the live interview. It's all we need.

I tell people to be on time and give themselves time to get lost. I let them know if they are late, they will not be let into the interview. Most of the people are there early but some of them show up late and guess what? They did not want the job strongly enough so I thank them for not wasting my time. I'm glad they showed me their true colors so I did not have to investigate further on my own. If someone is late to a job interview, they will be late to work; you can count on that with ABSOLUTE certainty!

During the interview, we are making lots of notes and I tell each candidate that they will receive an email from us within the next 24 hours. The email will say one of the following:

1. *Congratulations! You have been selected for the final round. Please join us at _____ for a cocktail mixer, and we give them the date, time and location of the final round of interviews or event.*

or

2. *We are sorry to inform you that you have not been selected for the position. Thank you for your time. We will keep your resume on file for future job openings.*

TG's Hot Tip ... Be kind and respectful of the time and effort that ALL of your candidates have put forth. Stick to your word and be sure that they get that email within 24 hours. I guarantee you that they are waiting by their inbox for the answer.

When I offer a letter of congratulations to a candidate, it's a BIG DEAL! At RMA our final round of interviews is typically at a cocktail mixer or some sort of special social event that's fun and full of high energy – it matches our culture! Make certain that your final interview process matches yours.

In the next chapter, I want to teach you my unique technique used for screening and interviewing high volume hires – a large number of people at one time – and salespeople. It's the BOMB extraordinaire!

Then, I'll be covering our signature process for the mixer in chapter 10, until then CHEERS!

9 | TG's CASTING CALL

I'd like to introduce you to the next technique used in the *Superstar Hiring System;* it's a unique process I created and I call it ... **The Casting Call**, better yet ... *TG's Casting Call!*

I guarantee that this is the first time you've heard of it! It's a process that I developed for filling openings in our **sales division** and for high volume hires.

This process works best for sales, and is also a good application for any job where you hire in large volume, hire for a position with a potential for a high rate of turnover, and for entry-level personnel.

Okay, here we go! The process **starts upon arrival** and I involve my front desk personnel as well. As each candidate arrives, they are first required to **sign-in** on a log sheet.

Second, they are **issued a number** — Their number is written on a badge, usually a "sticky badge." Now, and for the rest of the day, they are **referred to by their number.** *"Hello #8 ... it's nice to meet you!"*

TG's Hot Tip ... And by the way, nobody knows they are coming in for a **Casting Call**! Each applicant has been recently contacted by one of our staff members and *invited to come in for an interview at a specific time on a specific date.* If they can't make that time and date, they are told, "I'm sorry that's the only time slot available." Because **WHY?** Because ... HOW BADLY DO THEY WANT THIS JOB? Again, they have no idea it's a group of candidates on the same exact date and time!

Okay, back to the *Casting Call* process.

A typical *Casting Call* usually has about 20-25 candidates in the room. At the front of the room will be an executive panel, and in my business, it's made of myself, Ruby and all the branch managers.

Seated in front of us are rows and rows *and rows* of people that want to work for us.

Once everyone is seated we introduce ourselves and talk a little bit about the company and the position that they are applying for.

After that, it's time for **HOT SEATS!** I randomly pick a number and say, *"Number ___, come to the front of the room, tell us a little bit about yourself and why you would make an AMAZING Admissions Counselor!"*

TG's Hot Tip ... People that are shy are going to get sick with fear at this process. For me and the team, that's perfect! Because, guess what? I'm not looking for shy people!

If you are hiring for a sales position, you definitely need this process! It's a MUST DO.

Additionally and as I mentioned earlier, this process works if you hire in big numbers, have positions with a high rate of turnover, need to fill entry-level positions, or if you have multiple locations with similar positions that need to be filled and trained congruently.

It's a big time saver, and it offers great perspective as you watch the dynamics amongst the candidates, how they engage with each other, and how they interact with your current team.

During the *Casting Call* we are looking for specifics and making notes. We are watching the body language and listening to everything that the candidates *want* to tell us.

We are all making notes in the process so that we can confer later. We very purposely call on people at random and in no particular order so that they have no idea when it will be their time to stand in front of the room.

The entire live *Casting Call* process can take 60-90 minutes depending on how many people are in the room. After everyone has had a chance to step up and share their story, we ask if anyone else has anything they want to share before we step out of the room. There are times when people may want to add something, especially those that were the very first ones on the floor because honestly they kind of got screwed by having to go first! After they see everyone else speak, they think of a million ideas they wanted to share. Has that ever happened to you? Haha! Please give them an opportunity if they ASK for it! Remember, great sales people *always* ASK for the order.

The entire process is super fun! I'll keep saying it ... You really MUST add it to your hiring process in order to step up your hiring game!

We have become one of the most desirable places to work simply because it's so hard to get hired by us!

Once everyone is done sharing, the management panel steps out of the room to discuss the candidates. We like to crank up the music in the interview room and tell everyone to relax and mingle, and that we will be back in 15 minutes with our decisions. These are sales candidates, so they are usually outgoing and friendly people and they usually do get up and mix and mingle, and meet each other during the break.

In reality, our process of evaluation usually takes at least 30 minutes because all of us on the panel have to give our input about each candidate.

If you have more than one manager, they all need to be involved in the interview process. It should never be a solo process. There needs to be at least two decision makers that are involved.

For us, we know exactly who and what we are looking for. We know our avatar!

I can walk into that interview room, scan the crowd and know who I'm going to hire. But sure enough at every **Casting Call** there will be someone present that does NOT fit our profile, and yet they step up and totally blow me away with their confidence and clarity!

As the team and I are in the other room making decisions on who to hire, we are preparing numbered envelopes to hand each person when we return to the group. At this point, Ruby and I are done. We walk away and hand-off the final task to our Hiring Manager.

Then, the Hiring Manager walks back into the room and thanks everyone for coming out today. She proceeds to hold up the envelopes and says the following to those in attendance: *"Each of you will be getting an envelope today. Please don't open the envelope until you get into your car.*

The envelope will say one of two things: Congratulations, you've made it to the next round!" or, "We are sorry to inform you that you've not been selected today."

My manager will stand at the door way with the envelopes in her hand and give them to each person as they walk through the door to leave. Remember that each person is wearing a nametag with a number on it. They are given an envelope that matches their number. And YES we do double check the acceptance/decline letters before we put them in each envelope! So far we have never invited or declined the wrong person, but it could certainly happen.

What is the next round you might ask? Well, it's our signature mixer of course! This is our off the hook, fun event that you've never experienced if you are the typical employer who does random, boring interviews at your desk!

We spend A LOT of time and money during the process of the interview so that we narrow down the odds in our favor of picking the right person — the person that most likely fits our culture. I'd rather spend the time and money in the beginning rather than waste valuable time training the wrong person only to have to hire and retrain again.

TG's Hot Tip ... For a manager or key administrative position I skip the *Casting Call* and go straight to the one-on-one interview. The *Casting Call* has a specific application and usefulness in the hiring process, so use it efficiently and always to your best advantage.

10 | THE COCKTAIL MIXER

Well this is the moment that we've all been waiting for ... it's the COCKTAIL MIXER!

It's the highlight of the whole process and a key ingredient to my *Superstar Hiring System*.

ALL of the finalists move on to the cocktail mixer or social event where we have an absolute blast with our team and the potential new hires. Every job candidate ends up at a mixer; how they get there depends on what job they are applying for.

3. Sales Candidates are picked out of a *Casting Call*
4. Administrative and Management Candidates have passed interviews on the phone and via Skype

By now candidates have been narrowed down to the FAVORITE candidates. Maybe you THINK you know whom you're going to select from the live interviews, but this final phase is important to TRULY determine who fits the corporate culture of your company.

At RMA we set a date and time about a week in advance to give our final candidates the opportunity to move their calendar around so that they can attend. I usually pick 6:00 pm for the mixer so that everyone has a chance to finish their work day and drive to the designated location.

I can anticipate the mixer lasting 2 hours. Before the mixer I have been in touch with the management team at the venue to scope out a particular area inside where I want my group to meet up. Typically, I have already pre-designated an appetizer menu as well. Remember its six o'clock and people are coming straight from work.

Be fair to everyone in attendance ... give them some food, especially because it's a COCKTAIL mixer!

You might be wondering about the guest list. Who do we invite from our staff, and how many staff members do I bring to the mixer? I usually bring the branch manager and the entire team that will be working with the new hires.

The purpose of the mixer is for the team and the candidates to get to know each other on a social basis. It's an extremely informal job interview. It's an opportunity for people to talk about things they like and discover common interests with the team.

My team is very outgoing and is used to this process. More importantly, they talk to strangers for a living, so they are great in a mixer format of moving from person to person and just chatting and making great conversation with enthusiasm. Remember, our culture is based on that "feel good, I'm sexy, take over the world" mentality that empowers our team.

YOU will need to train your team the art of mingling at a mixer. It's important that nobody fixate on any one person for too long. At RMA we use the process for sales and we all network for a living, so having a mixer is a no brainer.

Our team loves it! It's fun that we get to work outside the office and have a cocktail too! My staff is standing in line, dying to be the one that gets to work the mixer! Be sure to have fun with it!

While I'm at the mixer, I move throughout the crowd the entire evening, connecting people. If I see candidates get stuck or feel somewhat alone, I'll connect them with a person or a group. As the team leader, I'm the only person in the room that knows EVERYONE so it's my job to keep it moving.

Throughout the mixer, Ruby and I stand back and watch the flow and body language of the people. We know it's difficult for people to be thrown to the lions like this. We are evaluating the flow and the ease of how the candidates move amongst our staff.

We think about all aspects of the interaction and ask ourselves questions like ..

- Do they fit in?
- Do they look like the Avatar?
- Do they feel like the Avatar?
- Will the Ruby Girls accept them into the team?

Have you ever seen the movie *"Mean Girls"* with Lindsay Lohan? It shows what happens when a newbie is dropped in with the popular girls - you don't want your new hires to be treated like this. #youcantsitwithus

As humans we are just naturally prone to form clicks with other people that mirror us. Make sure that your new hires fit the corporate culture and mirror the existing team. Trust me on this one; by now you DO trust me, right? It's a lot of work but the process is fun and well worth the time and money that goes into it.

Usually within 90 minutes, I can start to see the crowd winding down, losing interest, getting bored and tired. At this point I'll step in and bring it to an end. I thank the candidates for coming out, hug them good night and let them know that they will receive an email tomorrow with our decision.

Immediately after the candidates depart, we get the staff together and converse about the evening. Topics of discussion include:

- What did we see?
- Who did we like?
- Who fits the avatar mold?
- Who is absolutely NOT the avatar?

We usually spend about 30 minutes in this process.

It's important that the team be united in this decision. We don't just bring them in for fun. We really want them to be involved in the hiring process. We are all natural born sales people so we go back and forth working to sway each other that OUR choice is the right choice! In the end, we always agree and happily pick our new hires together.

The mixer is an absolute mandatory process. Sometimes I feel like I know who I'm going to hire but I never know for sure until I see them mix with the team and get the stamp of approval from the hiring team.

I want to re-emphasize that you have told ALL the candidates that they will get an email from you tomorrow. It's really important that you follow up and send every single person an email with the decision, good or bad. You have to realize that by this point, they are waiting by their computer to find out whether or not they got the job!

I really hope you embrace this key step as we have. It's proven to be a tremendous asset to our process and our organization.

With that in mind, your very last homework assignment for **TG's Superstar Hiring System** will be to find a venue to host your events.

TG's Hot Tip ... It's important that you can have a private section. You cannot be dropped into the middle of happy hour in the center of the bar. Take the time to look around your neighborhood at your choices. Sometimes I use a small local eatery, other times I use a big national franchise chain. It just depends on the bar and restaurant management, and their desire to work with you.

Good luck and have fun with this homework assignment. It gives you a legitimate reason to restaurant and bar hop, *and* make it a tax deduction!

11 | IT'S A WRAP

Well we made it to the end! Congratulations and thank you for sticking it out and making the commitment to your success and finding your SUPERSTAR HIRE!

Let's recap what we've learned:

1. Culture has EVERYTHING to do with hiring!
2. You created an Avatar of your business.
3. You assessed your corporate environment, thoroughly dissected it and have a true understanding of exactly who will work best inside of your organization.
4. The key resources to finding your Avatar are:
    a. Social Media - Facebook and Instagram
    b. Classified ads - use www.Indeed.com
    c. Employee referrals with incentives
5. Process of Elimination
    a. Screen resumes quickly and sort
    b. Look for candidates in social media because we can learn more from a Facebook page than we will in a job interview

Trish Grimes

    c. Follow my ***Secret Formula for Screening Success*** and look for relevance

6. Telephone Interviews
    a. A 3 minute phone chat tells you if they are:
        - Smart
        - Motivated
        - Excited
        - Lazy
        - Funny
    b. Take great notes!
    c. Eliminate or pass them onto the Video Chat

7. Video Chat via SKYPE
    a. Now you can SEE who's on the other end of that resume - How do they show up?
    b. Your finalists from here are granted a live interview

8. Live Interviews
    a. Candidates interview one by one in front of your hiring panel every 15 minutes
    b. Top contenders are invited to the cocktail mixer

9. TG's Casting Call
    a. Candidates interview in a group and are called one by one in front of your hiring panel every 15 minutes
    b. Top contenders are invited to the cocktail mixer

52

10. Cocktail Mixer, Mixer or Social Event
    a. Staff and job candidates all come together to mix and mingle and decide who will be joining your team
    b. What matters most is that everyone involved in the decision is there
    c. When it comes to a mixer, the more, the merrier!
11. Make that **SUPERSTAR HIRE!**
    a. At the end of the mixer you get together with all your staff and pick the next round of new hires!
    b. Your **YES** file should now be full of your *Superstar Hires!*

It's just that simple!

I truly hope you enjoyed learning my *Superstar Hiring System* filled with all of the stellar strategies, proprietary methods, and my *TG's Hot Tips* for hiring success.

By now you should be motivated to implement everything right away in your own business, and if you've completed each assignment, you are well on your way to building a solid team by making the **RIGHT SUPERSTAR HIRE!**

This system has helped me to create a multi-million dollar **INC. 500/5000** company and I know it will help you too!

Trish Grimes

| MEET THE AUTHOR

TRISH GRIMES

*CFO & Vice President of Ruby Studios, Inc.
& Ruby Makeup Academy*

Founder & CEO of Trish Grimes Consulting

http://TrishGrimes.com

Trish Grimes makes HIRING SUPERSTARS an absolute breeze with her proprietary strategies and systems for success. For over 20 years in Corporate America she is best known for creating a multi-million dollar enterprise as CFO & Vice President of Ruby Studios, Inc., and Ruby Makeup Academy — an INC. 500/5000 Company, and one of the largest makeup schools in the World.

Thanks to her ingenuity, creating an ideal corporate culture, and producing a raving fan base of superstar employees known as Ruby Girls, Trish strictly hires the best of the best!

As a dynamic Keynote Speaker, Trish shares her versatile and unique approach to operations and hiring principles with corporate teams, executive boards and small business owners nationwide. Her raw, no frills, no fluff approach is well respected and easily implemented in American business.

Trish Grimes Consulting is her newest venture, and as Founder and CEO she brings honesty, integrity and real life experience to the boardroom. She knows what it takes to build a profitable brand, create a successful and memorable image, *and* build a solid team of superstar employees that breed big sales, productivity and enthusiasm in a highly competitive marketplace.

Her personal and professional experiences — knowing what works well and what does not — mixed with her savvy, ambitious personality simply compliments her formal education and specialty training; especially behind the scenes of any business.

"Systemize, strategize and create a dream team for your company."
- TG

TRISH GRIMES

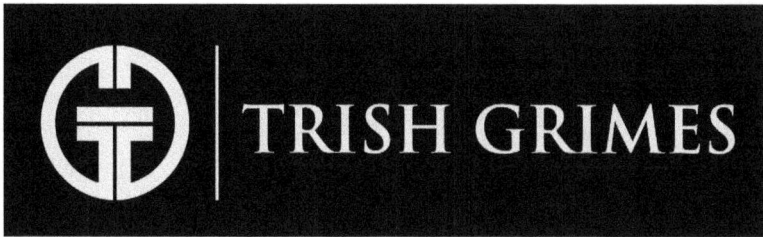

Trish Grimes, CPSC earned her Bachelor of Arts in Business Administration from California State University San Bernardino, and graduated from the Success Coach Institute as a Certified Professional Success Coach.

She loves making money for herself, her companies, and her clients! Early in her career and before moving into the beauty and education industry, Trish had a booming real estate business. She excels in the principles of business and finance, respects it, and she simply *knows* how to grow bottom line profits fast and efficiently. She credits that her stellar track record of big wins starts with a solutions-driven approach and is complimented by her keen sense of solid operations — It's the perfect mix to living the life of her dreams and the life of financial freedom!

Be sure to stay connected with Trish Grimes and get her latest updates and invitations to events, trainings and specialty programs. Visit her online, or connect and follow Trish via social media...

http://TrishGrimes.com
https://www.facebook.com/trishgrimesbusinesspage
https://www.instagram.com/grimes2trish/

www.ingramcontent.com/pod-product-compliance
Lightning Source LLC
Chambersburg PA
CBHW071122210326
41519CB00020B/6386